THAI COOKING
in a Sufi's Kitchen

by Alima Ravadi Quinn

A Continuation of "Joy of Thai Cooking"

Emerald of Siam Publishing

This book is dedicated to
My beloved Master Hidayat Inayat Khan
who reminds me of my true nature

And

To the memory of

My first teachers of love,
my parents, by their loving example

And

Mother Marie Therese Morganty
who reflected Christ's love in her loving care to me
when I was in Australia

Also

Sri Nisargadatta Maharaj whose inspiring teaching has
illuminated my mind

And

Rumi the great poet of the 13th Century whose poetry
has ripened (opened) my heart forever

ACKNOWLEDGEMENTS

To Sorasak Lekprichakul for financing this book.

To Alim Garry, the man in my life, who chose me to be the mother of his children, and whom I chose to be the father of our children. He has been my English tutor for almost 40 years. I enjoy the opportunity he gave me to learn about America and the rich cultures of those who have come here from different parts of the world. This has enriched my life in the last 36 years.

To my son-in-law Rob Burroughs, for editing "The Message from the Author" which is the inspiration for the birth of this book.

To my daughter Suzanne Burroughs, for her graphic design talent and for providing me with enough computer knowledge to do this cookbook.

To my son Bill, for taking full responsibility for the Emerald of Siam while this book was in process in Thailand.

To my youngest daughter Dara (means star in Thai), for her kind thoughts about me and also for editing the final draft of all my recipes.

To Ray O'Halloran, for proof-reading the first draft of my recipes.

To my Emerald customers, for their commitment to buy this book while it was still in the writing process. Their support was another source of confidence and inspiration, which enabled me to finish the project.

To my sisters Sunanta, Supanee, and Angela, to my brother Sorasak and his wife Napha, also to my brother Surachai and his wife Soontree, for their assistance and loving care when I was in Bangkok while the book was in the printing process.

To Virda Nunn for her proof-reading skills to finish this book. (She's amazing!)

And to you, of course, who now own this book. I wish you a very joyful time with Thai cooking, and eating with mindfulness. May it bring you a happy, healthy, and meaningful life.

CONTENTS

MESSAGE FROM THE AUTHOR

Love Is All

Before I entered my mother's womb,
  I knew only love.
    How can I forget love,
      when I was created by love, to love,
          and be loved.

-Alima Ravadi Quinn

I was inspired to write this poem after my initiation as a Sufi by Master Hidayat Inayat Kahn in 1995.

The Message I shared with my first Thai cookbook, "Joy of Thai Cooking" published in 1990, was of my early childhood experiences in Thai culture with food.

With this book, I wish to share my recent deep insights about the loving relationship of my body with food.

My relationship with food began to change after my initiation as a Sufi and I had begun the practice of giving full mindfulness and attention to my spiritual life. With my growing spiritual awareness came a clearer awareness of my body's own wisdom concerning its needs.

My time spent in the kitchen of the Thai restaurant, co-founded in 1983 by my sister Sunanta Kulthol (now retired and living, once again, in Thailand) and me, began to bring new meaning to my life. The kitchen has become a place of reverence and meditation, a place for the practice of love, much more than just a place of work or obligation.

In the preparation of fresh vegetables, I found a new sense of beauty and proportion. I realized the shape, color, and size of the vegetables could enhance the loving quality being revealed in the food being prepared.

A sense of joy and gratitude toward all life began to be my focus. A new attitude about cooking began to emerge. This sacrifice of life for life, the joyous contribution these ingredients made, allowing for the joyous continuation of the human race through the consumption of this food, gave me great peace.

As humans, we have been given the great gift of choosing to enjoy life on this planet. Food is one of the most important choices we make each day. Food serves not only to nourish and to keep us alive physically, but also to entertain and to bring us great pleasure in the enjoyment of smelling, tasting, and eating these treasures of life prepared with love, care, and artistry.

I believe we all have inside of us a wisdom that knows exactly what our body needs. As a greater awareness of this inner wisdom grows, we gain a clearer intuition of how we can satisfy that need with each meal we consume.

I began to realize a healthy meal prepared with loving energy, with full attention to the presentation and balance of flavors, will create a hidden nutritional value to the body. The loving, caring energy carried in the food will stimulate the body to function in balance and harmony. All of the natural functions of the body will be nourished, and the spirit will be invigorated.

I feel sad to see people in the most advanced of societies paying so little attention to the real needs of the body, preferring to leave the care of the body to medical experts after the body functions are so out of balance that a disease appears.

I see our bodies as little children who need our loving attention and care. We need to allow our inner wisdom to give them love with the food they eat, to watch them as they play, and to hug them when they need love. With loving nourishment, our little children will grow beautifully throughout their lives. Healthy bodies will enhance healthy minds to create beauty, love, and peace. The body and mind will live in peace together as best of friends in joyful harmony always.

To this day, I remember the sound of my mother's voice as she would say to me, "I can feed only your body and not your mind." If she were here today, I know she would be so happy to see the results of her loving care for my body, with food provided and filled with love.

I know she would be pleased that the food she fed me, to help in the development of my healthy body and mind, allowed me to grow over time into a person able to enjoy and to live a wonderful, happy, and meaningful life.

I offer this message in the hope it will be an inspiration for you to pay more attention to your body's own needs and inner wisdom, that they might grow in health, peace, love, and joy.

With my best wishes, I share another poem…

Teach Your Child Only Love

Teach your child only love;
Your child was born with Divine grace to love and be loved.

Teach your child only love;
Only love can give your child passion for living.

Teach your child only love;
Only love can connect you to your child's soul.

Teach your child only love;
Only love can overcome your child's fear.

Teach your child only love;
Only love can teach your child forgiveness.

Teach your child only love;
Only love can witness God's presence to your child.

Teach your child only love;
Only love can make your child whole.

-Alima Ravadi Quinn

What Is Thai Food?

I have often been asked to explain the difference between Thai and Chinese food. The best answer I can offer is this: when you go to a Chinese restaurant, you will not taste Thai flavors; but if you go to a Thai restaurant, you will find some Chinese flavors. Thai food is a blend of many cultures.

The recent introduction of Thai cuisine to the West has brought to world attention one of the most prized cultural contributions of this once-isolated land. It is no longer a hidden treasure. With the close of the Vietnam War and the exile of a multitude of refugees from Southeast Asia, Thailand began exporting the necessary ingredients to prepare Thai cuisine. Although Vietnamese and Thai cuisine share many of the same ingredients, it is the unique Thai style of preparation that gives Thai food its character.

After 1976, Thai citizens in the United States began opening Thai restaurants. Soon there were Thai restaurants in cities all across the nation. I was inspired to participate in sharing the beauty of the Thai culture here in America. With seed money from my parents, my sister and I opened the Emerald of Siam in 1983 in Richland, Washington. With the help of three of my children, it remains a thriving business to this day.

I selected mostly traditional Thai recipes for this book, but I have included personal recipes, as well. I have always found inspiration by quieting my mind and being "at one" with the kitchen. The results are such recipes as Smoked Salmon Fried Rice (page 119), as well as many of the vegetarian dishes included in this book.

Wonderful ingredients prepared with loving care create a beautiful and delicious meal, and will contribute joy and good health to our lives. As Buddha taught 2500 years ago, good health is the most valuable quality in life.

I offer you these recipes so that with these delights of Thai cuisine, you might enjoy your life with equal attention to mind, body, and soul.

The following are some quotes about what Thai food is to some people who have been enjoying Thai food for many years, either as customers of our restaurant, The Emerald of Siam, or by cooking Thai food for themselves:

"Thai food expands taste horizons and enriches the soul."
-Rev. Jim and Kathy Dyson

"Healthy food with comforting textures --- not pretentious --- but nevertheless one of the richest cuisines on earth!"
-Tim Scheibe

"Thai food is home cooking, and the Emerald is home."
-Bill Blakeman

"Thai cuisine is exotic and allows me to travel in my dreams to far away places."
-Lynn Arden

"Cooking Thai food has enriched my life with its tantalizing flavors, dishing out a little love with every plate."
-Deanna Bierwirth

"The visual image, the aroma, the taste; In these delights of Thai meals, I burst into song..."
-Janet Tyler

"Thai food is the bridge between body and soul."
-Ravadi Quinn

"To you it might be *Thai food*. To me it's just *food.*"
-Bill Quinn

"The many dishes of Thai Cuisine reveal the inner flavors of the heart."

-Robert Burroughs

Illusion And Grace

With all the wealth that the world has to offer me,

It will never match what God has given me.

The world can only offer me what I need to survive as a human being,

But God offers me His Wisdom to live as a Divine Being.

The world can only offer me hope to have a good life,

But God offers His Living in me.

The world can only offer me the beauty of illusion,

But God offers His Vision for me to see the Beauty of Reality.

The world can only offer me beautiful places to attain peace,

But God offers His Grace to bring me Peace.

-Alima Ravadi Quinn

GUIDE TO THAI INGREDIENTS AND UTENSILS

or

"Toys In Your Playground"

Do not allow the unfamiliar Thai ingredients to intimidate you. Get to know your new ingredients. Visit the Asian store in your neighborhood if there is one. Make friends with them; bring a copy of the cookbook so that you can show them pictures of what you are looking for. Just like toys in a playground, cooking ingredients are meant to be used, explored, and enjoyed. As in life itself, Thai cooking does not have to be taken so seriously. Inquisitively experiment with the new ingredients you will be using.

Allow yourself to try Thai food at any Thai restaurant whenever you travel to different cities, so you may compare it to what you have in your own town. Take Thai cooking classes when there is an opportunity. From these experiences, you will find yourself becoming more creative with your senses. It is a good way to expand the comfort zone of all your senses.

The amount of seasoning indicated in each recipe is a guideline, intended to be increased or decreased according to your taste. Pay attention to the flavors of each dish while adjusting the seasoning to your taste. Your body can help you find the right balance for your palate. "It is a little piece of heaven served on a plate" according to long-time Emerald customers Mr. & Mrs. W. Smith of Benton City.

There is no need for you to look for any particular utensils for Thai cooking. An electric rice cooker is the only utensil which I consider very useful for anyone interested in Asian cooking since most Oriental dishes are served with steamed rice.

The following ingredients are used in various recipes in this book. Make friends with them, as you will encounter one or more of them in almost every recipe.

Bamboo Shoots: Young bamboo plants are harvested when they are still soft. You can purchase these in cans in the Asian section of your local grocery store or in Asian markets. These shoots are used in curry dishes as a substitute for Thai eggplant.

Bean Sauce: This sauce is preserved whole soya-bean. It is salty, but with flavor. Used in Pahd See-lw. Use sparingly.

Bean Threads: These clear noodles are made from mung beans. They are available dried in small packages in chain grocery stores.

Bean Curd or Tofu: Several kinds are found in Asian markets. They are also available in health food stores.

Black Rice: This unique rice is imported from Thailand and is available in Asian markets.

Black Mushroom: Buy it dried in strips or whole - also known as Shitake.

Chili Paste or Nam Prik Pao: Translated literally as "roasted curry paste," this essential can be purchased from Asian markets. Usually packed in a jar, it is used in Lemon Grass Soup. It is also tasty enough to season hot steamed rice when you are too hungry to take the time to prepare a meal [a good idea for single men or women].

Chili Pepper: Thai hot pepper is available in any Asian store. You can freeze them whole for later use.

Chili Sauce: This sauce is made from red chili, vinegar, and garlic. The most famous brand is Sriracha brand which is named after the town Srirircha, Thailand where it was produced.

Chinese Parsley: Also known as cilantro or coriander, this useful herb has several edible and aromatic parts. People in Thailand use the roots for seasoning, and the leaves for salad and garnish.

Coconut Cream (Milk): In Thailand, we buy freshly grated coconut to prepare for the curry or desserts; but outside of Thailand, the imported canned coconut cream (13.5 oz) serves very well for this book's recipes.

Curry Paste: There are many kinds of curry in complete Thai cuisine. Only five are introduced in this book: green curry, red curry, yellow curry, massamun curry, and panang curry. All are available in Asian markets across the USA. *Please take my advice, and do not try to make your own curry paste. The imported Thai curry pastes are prepared by specialists. Most Thai cooks also buy their curry paste ready-made!*

Dry Rice Noodles: These noodles are sold in small, medium, and large widths in Asian markets. If the market is out of the size you need, don't be afraid to experiment with another.

Fish Sauce: This sauce is used in Thai cuisine almost as freely as soy sauce is used in Chinese cooking. Each brand has a different salt content. Proportions in this book are based on the "Thai" brand.

Fried Garlic: It is now available imported from Thailand in a jar. It is used for Garlic Chicken and Garlic Tofu recipes. Available at any Asian market.

Fried Tofu: There are several kinds available in health food or Asian food stores. You want a kind that will absorb better; they usually come in a sheet and are kept in the refrigerated area. You can freeze fried tofu for later use.

Galangal: This ginger-like root is available fresh, dry, powdered, or frozen in most Asian groceries.

Granulated Garlic: As found in the spice section of your local grocery store, make sure it is not garlic salt, just garlic.

Jasmine Rice: White long grain rice is imported from Thailand. After you have tried Thai jasmine rice, you will not be happy with any other long grain rice.

Kaffir Lime Leaves: This is an important herb in preparing curry dishes (just like bay leaves to spaghetti sauce). Can be purchased dry or frozen in Asian markets.

Lemon Grass: This is another essential Thai herb, which is used in Thai curry paste. It can be purchased fresh, frozen, and in powder form in any Asian grocery store. I have been told that lemon grass is very good for the nervous system. It is used in two well-known Thai soups, Tom Yum Goong (page 21) and Tom Kha Gai (page 25).

Oyster Sauce: This sauce is used in most stir-fry dishes. Available in most grocery store chains.

Pahd Thai Noodles: They are dried medium-width rice noodles (the width is really up to you).

Preserved Turnip: This imported delicacy will never be found in your neighborhood salad bar! It comes in 1-pound packages. Choose the already chopped one. Wash well before use. Keep the rest in a jar, refrigerated. It is called for in the recipe for Pahd Thai found in this book.

Rice Paper Wrappers: Some big chain stores now carry them in the Asian food section. Make sure they are not all broken up before purchase. They are sold dried in a package and are usually round and flat in shape - the diameter of a large pancake.

Roasted Ground Rice: This rice is a very important ingredient in making Larb Gai and Larb Tofu. I recommend home-made. A recipe follows at the end of this ingredients list.

Sour Shrimp Paste: This paste can be used in Vegetarian Lemon Grass Soup. Make sure to read the label because some brands have no shrimp content.

Sticky Rice or Sweet Rice: Glutinous rice is a staple diet of Laos and the Eastern part of Thailand. In Bangkok, Thais use it in a variety of desserts.

Tamarind Juice: This is an important seasoning agent in massamun curry, peanut sauce, and the main "secret" of Pahd Thai. Now you can purchase the Tamarind concentrate in a can, instead of having to get the juice out of the Tamarind fruit, as in my previous book, "Joy of Thai Cooking."

Thai Basil: This fragrant relative of common basil is used in most curry and stir-fry dishes. It can be purchased year-round in Asian markets in most big cities across the USA.

Thai Soy Sauce: This flavored soy sauce carries the brand name "Golden Mountain Sauce." It is imported from Thailand.

Wood-Ear Mushroom: Sometimes this mushroom is called black fungus (available dried in the Asian food section at the large chain stores or at an Asian market).

ROASTED GROUND RICE

Ingredients:
1   cup long grain sweet rice (raw)
¼ cup fresh or dry galangal
¼ cup fresh or dry lemon grass
4   fresh or dry kaffir lime leaves

Method:
1. In a skillet, over medium heat, sauté the four ingredients until the mixture turns dark brown (almost black). Remove from heat. Let cool.
2. In a blender, on high speed, grind the mixture until it is very fine (almost a powder). Store in a tight jar for future use. This recipe is used in the Larb Gai (page 47) and Larb Tofu (page 83) recipes in this book.

Just Love Me

I am very fragile, like a child.
I can only take one step at a time.
Do not push me or pull me.
Encourage me if you can; if you can't,
Just love me.

I am very new to the world.
When I am lost and ask for help,
Don't tell me what I should have done.
Help me if you can; if you can't,
Just love me.

My emotions are my birthright,
So I may experience my human limitation.
When I am in fear or in pain,
Hold me, or listen to me if you can; if you can't,
Just love me.

Innocence is my divine nature.
When I enjoy what I like to do,
Don't interrupt and take it away from me.
If you do, both of us will need to be healed.
Just loving me is not enough.

-Alima Ravadi Quinn

SOUP AND SALAD

Lemon Grass Shrimp Soup (Tom Yum Goong)

Bean Thread Soup

Galangal Chicken Soup (Tom Kha Gai)

Beef Noodle Soup (Pho')

Cucumber Soup

Beef Salad (Yum Nuea)

Cucumber Salad

Emerald Salad With House Dressing

Green Papaya Salad (Som Tum)

Thai Tuna Salad

LEMON GRASS SHRIMP SOUP (Tom Yum Goong)

A classic soup, used in many Thai homes for entertaining guests. Over the years, it has been a cold-remedy for many of my guests at the Emerald. This soup is very low in calories.

4 servings

Ingredients:
16 large prawns
1 tablespoon chili paste
2 tablespoons fresh lime juice (or to taste)
1 tablespoon fish sauce (or to taste)
1 stalk fresh lemon grass, cut into small slices (use only the white part)
4 fresh kaffir lime leaves
2 fresh hot chili peppers (optional)
½ cup sliced fresh mushrooms
8 whole baby corn, cut in halves lengthwise
1 medium tomato cut into 4 wedges
6 cups chicken stock
¼ cup sliced fresh galangal
¼ cup chopped cilantro for garnish

Method:
1. Peel and de-vein the prawns; keep the tails on. Set aside.
2. Bring chicken stock to a boil.
3. Add kaffir lime leaves, lemon grass, galangal, mushrooms, and baby corn. Boil for 3 minutes.
4. In a small bowl, mix chili paste, fish sauce, and lime juice with a spoon until the mixture is well-blended. Put it aside.
5. Add prawns and tomato wedges into the boiling broth, cooking until the shrimp turn pink. Add the seasoning mixture. Bring the soup to a boil again.
6. Remove from heat. Transfer to a serving bowl. Garnish with cilantro.

Note: If you like the soup spicier, add the chili pepper 1 minute before removing it from heat.

BEAN THREAD SOUP

A low-fat diet soup. Very easy to prepare. Only a few ingredients make a very delightful bowl of soup.

4 servings

Ingredients:
¼ pound bean threads soaked in cold water until soft
8 cups clear chicken broth
2 tablespoons light soy sauce
½ cup fresh sliced mushroom
2 green onions, cut into sections (optional)
½ cup boneless ground chicken or lean ground pork, seasoned with
1 teaspoon sesame oil
1 teaspoon fish sauce and ¼ teaspoon black pepper

Method:
1. Cut bean threads into 5-inch long sections.
2. In a small saucepan, add two cups water, bring to a boil over high heat.
3. Add the seasoned chicken or pork, as desired, to the boiling water. Stir until the meat is cooked. Remove from heat. Rest the meat in a strainer. Discard the water.
4. In a large saucepan, add chicken broth to the saucepan. Bring the broth to a boil over high heat. Add mushrooms, bean threads, and meat. Vegetarians, leave out the meat. Bring the food mixture to a boil. Add light soy sauce to taste.
5. Add green onions and black pepper. Remove from heat. Serve at once.

Note: If you want this soup to be the whole meal for lunch, just add more bean threads to the soup during cooking, or serve with steamed rice.

GALANGAL CHICKEN SOUP (Tom Kha Gai)

Another classic Thai soup. It is rich enough to make as a main course when served with steamed rice. Vegetarians may substitute fresh tofu for the chicken.

4 servings

Ingredients:
1 cup cut-up chicken breast, or ¼ pound of fresh tofu, cut into small cubes (½ inch)
1 can coconut milk (13.5 oz.)
2 cups chicken broth (vegans can use water instead)
½ cup sliced fresh mushrooms
4 kaffir lime leaves
2 stalks lemon grass (cut into 1-inch sections)
1 big chunk galangal, sliced
2-3 tablespoons fish sauce (or to taste)
¼ cup fresh lime juice (or to taste)
4 fresh chili peppers, sliced in half
¼ cup chopped cilantro

Method:
1. Heat chicken broth in a large saucepan. Bring to a boil.
2. Add chicken, galangal, kaffir lime leaves, and lemon grass. Bring broth back to a boil and cook until the chicken meat is cooked. Vegetarians may use tofu, but add it later.
3. Add coconut milk. Vegetarians may now add the tofu. Bring to a boil.
4. Add the fish sauce, lime juice, and the fresh chili (to taste).
5. Remove from heat, garnish with cilantro. Serve at once.

BEEF NOODLE SOUP (Pho')

Pho', a well-known Vietnamese noodle soup dish. It is a very popular home-prepared soup, but is also popular in restaurants and with food vendors in Thailand. You can find instant Pho' in small packages in Asian grocery stores. It is very convenient for a fast meal, but I would dress the soup up with some meat and fresh vegetables to make it more enjoyable and to let your body know that you care. You will need 2 packages to make a full meal. To make the soup more appealing, I cook the noodles separately from the seasoning to keep the soup clear from starch.

1 serving

Ingredients:
2 oz. cooked beef strips (can be leftover steak)
2 packages Pho' rice noodles
1 cup bean sprouts
½ cup fresh basil leaves (optional)
4 cups clear chicken broth
2 green onions, chopped (optional)
½ tablespoon fried garlic

Method:
1. In a large soup bowl, soak the noodles with hot water for a few minutes. Drain and return the noodles to the soup bowl.
2. Blanch the bean sprouts with hot water if you don't like to have them in your soup fresh. Add the bean sprouts on top of the noodles.
3. Add meat, green onion, basil, and fried garlic.
4. Bring the chicken broth to a boil in a saucepan; add seasoning packets from noodles, stir, and mix well.
5. Remove from heat. Add the broth to the noodle mixture. Serve hot.

Note: You may substitute with another kind of vegetable if you do not care for bean sprouts. To enhance the flavors, I always add 2 tablespoons vinegar with hot pepper.

CUCUMBER SOUP

One of my family's favorite soups for lunch or dinner. If you are vegetarian, you can omit the meat and add some fresh mushrooms instead.

4 servings

Ingredients:
¼ pound ground chicken breast, mixed well with ¼ teaspoon black pepper, ¼ teaspoon sesame oil, and ½ teaspoon light soy sauce
1 large or 2 small cucumbers, seeded after cutting in half and quartering, sliced into 1-inch long segments
6 cups clear chicken stock
1 teaspoon fish sauce
1 teaspoon light soy sauce
¼ cup chopped green onion (optional)

Method:
1. In a saucepan, bring chicken broth to a boil.
2. Drop in ground chicken mixture with a teaspoon, 1 teaspoon at a time, until it is used up.
3. Cook meat until the soup comes to a boil again. Add cucumber and seasoning.
4. As soon as the chicken is cooked, remove from heat. Transfer the soup to a soup tureen or four individual soup bowls.

Note: You may make the 4 servings into a full meal for yourself with hot steamed rice.

BEEF SALAD (Yum Nuea)

A light meal to serve if you are not too hungry. A good salad to take to a party.

8 servings

Ingredients:
½ pound top sirloin
2 tablespoons fish sauce
2 tablespoons fresh lime juice
1 tablespoon chili paste(optional)

Salad Mix:
1 small cucumber, sliced
1 small onion, sliced
1 small tomato, sliced
1 small head Iceberg lettuce, cut into 2-inch pieces
½ cup fresh mint leaves
½ tablespoon, or more, ground chili pepper (or to taste)
½ cup sliced fresh mushroom

Method:
1. Cut meat into thin slices. Set aside.
2. To prepare the sauce: mix fish sauce, lime juice, chili paste, and chili pepper in small bowl. Mix well and set aside.
3. Cook the meat in a heated sauce pan, stirring until meat is no longer red. Remove from heat. Add sauce to the meat. Mix well.
4. Combine the meat with the salad and mix until it is well-blended.

Note: If desired, make more sauce to add to the salad. If you are taking it to a party, do not mix the meat into the salad until you are ready to serve.

CUCUMBER SALAD

A salad usually served as a condiment to Satay, Indian Style Curry, and Fish-Cakes. It is a good friend of peanut sauce.

4 servings

Ingredients:
2   cucumbers, peeled, cut in half lengthwise, then sliced
½ cup sugar
½ cup white vinegar
½ teaspoon salt
¼ cup ground roasted peanuts (optional)
¼ cup diced shallots (optional)

Method:
1. Put prepared cucumbers in serving bowl. Top with shallots.
2. In a saucepan, add sugar, vinegar, and salt. Heat over high heat. Stir until the mixture comes to a boil. Simmer for a few minutes, or until sugar is well-dissolved.
3. Remove from heat and let cool. Pour over cucumbers. Top with ground peanuts.

EMERALD SALAD WITH HOUSE DRESSING

Very popular at the Emerald of Siam Restaurant. I am often asked for the recipe of this dressing. It is very light. There is no oil involved.

8 servings

Ingredients:
1   small head Iceberg lettuce, cut up
½ cup sliced fresh mushrooms
½ cup sliced onion
½ cup sliced cucumber
2   small tomatoes, sliced
2   cups fresh spinach

Method:
1. In a large salad serving bowl, arrange salad mixture, starting with a layer of Iceberg lettuce on the bottom, then spinach, onion, fresh mushrooms, sliced cucumber, and tomato slices.
2. Pour the house dressing evenly (to taste, there will be extra) over the top of the salad. Toss the salad before serving.

HOUSE DRESSING

Ingredients:
1   cup vinegar
1   cup sugar
1   teaspoon paprika

1   tablespoon fresh lime juice
1   teaspoon salt
1   tablespoon fish sauce

Method:
1. In a sauce pan, bring vinegar and sugar to a boil. Stir and mix well.
2. Add salt. Lower heat to low. Simmer until sugar is well-dissolved and it becomes syrup-like. Let cool.
3. Add fish sauce, lime juice, and paprika. Serve over salad, as needed.

GREEN PAPAYA SALAD (Som Tum)

A popular salad from the Eastern Region of Thailand. We have been asked frequently if we had it on the menu. Green papaya is not easy to find in small towns all year-round. If you can find it in the Asian market where you live, it will be well worth the time spent finding it and preparing Som Tum for yourself!

4 servings

Ingredients:
1   small green papaya (make sure that it is hard when you squeeze it), shredded into 3-inch long strips
4   cloves fresh garlic
3   tablespoons dried shrimp (available in Asian market)
2   fresh hot chili pepper (add more if you like it hotter)
4   tablespoons fresh lime juice (or to taste)
1   tablespoon fish sauce (or to taste)
1   teaspoon sugar
2   tablespoons coarsely ground peanuts
4   cherry tomatoes
1   cup fresh green beans, cut into 2-inch pieces

Method:
1. In a large mortar, grind garlic, dried shrimp, hot chili pepper, and green beans with a pestle. Mix well with a large spoon.
2. Add the green papaya and cherry tomatoes. Grind with pestle and mix with a long spoon until the mixture is well-blended.
3. Mix in the lime juice, fish sauce, sugar, and peanuts. Mix well with the papaya.
4. Remove to a serving platter. Serve with sticky rice.

THAI TUNA SALAD

An easy and tasty way to serve tuna from a can. It is one of my son's comfort foods. I always enjoy preparing this dish for him. I know that whenever he asks for this dish, his body needs some attention. It is good for lunch, as well as for dinner, when you are not too hungry. It is very light, but very satisfying.

4 servings

Ingredients:
2 cans (6.5 oz.) solid white tuna, packed in water
4 tablespoons fresh lime juice
1½ tablespoons fish sauce
1 small onion, sliced
¼ teaspoon black pepper
½ teaspoon ground hot chili pepper (or to taste)
¼ cup chopped green onion
¼ cup cilantro (optional)

Method:
1. Discard excess water from the tuna.
2. Add all ingredients.
3. Mix well. Serve on lettuce, or hot steamed rice, or rice crackers.

Heaven And Earth

My father is a shining light from Heaven.
My mother is a sacred gift from the Earth.

My father gave me his global vision.
My mother gave me her earthly wisdom.

My father taught me courage by his failure.
My mother gave me courage by her liberal womanhood.

My father taught me acceptance by his tolerance.
My mother's unconditional love made me feel accepted.

My father's vision lighted my path.
My mother's wisdom nurtured my confidence.

My father taught me freedom of the mind.
My mother taught me the power of an open heart.

When my father passed away,
He left me with a beautiful path to continue.

When my mother left her body,
She left a gift of wholeness in my heart.

-Alima Ravadi Quinn

APPETIZERS

Thai Spring Rolls

Larb Gai

Emerald Butterflies

Spicy Fish-Cakes

Chicken Satay With Peanut Sauce

Crispy Yum-Yums

Emerald Chicken Wings

THAI SPRING ROLLS

Spring rolls - very welcome at any potluck party. They hold up much better than the vegetarian-style ones.

2 dozen

Ingredients:
2 dozen spring roll wrappers
½ pound ground chicken breast
2 small bundles (2 oz. each) dried bean threads, soaked in cold water
1 cup fresh bean sprouts
4 cups shredded green cabbage
½ cup chopped onion
½ cup shredded carrot
½ cup prepared wood-ear mushrooms, shredded
½ cup green peas
1 tablespoon Emerald Stir-Frying Sauce (page 134)
1 egg
1 teaspoon white pepper, mix with 1 teaspoon salt and 1 teaspoon sugar
2 tablespoons tapioca starch, mix with ½ cup hot water, to form a paste to seal the spring rolls
vegetable oil for deep frying

Method:
1. Remove bean threads from the water, cut each bundle in half.
2. Blanch the bean threads in boiling water. Remove with a strainer as soon as all the bean threads are under hot water. Set aside to cool.
3. Return the water to a boil, add cabbage, and cook for 1 minute. Remove cabbage from water with a strainer. Set aside to cool.
4. In a large mixing bowl, mix all ingredients starting with chicken, onion, carrot, green peas, mushroom, egg, pepper, sugar, salt, and Emerald Stir-Frying Sauce. Mix well first, then add the bean threads. Mix well. Mix in cabbage and follow with bean sprouts. *(See illustration on next page.)*
5. Deep fry the rolls in hot oil about 350 degrees until golden brown.

Note: Please make sure the oil is not over-heated, as the wrapper will burn before the meat is cooked inside.

HOW TO MAKE SPRING ROLLS - part 1

1. Your prepared stuffing, the tapioca starch mixture with a brush and your spring roll wrappers.

2. Lay one wrapper on a clean flat surface. (The one in the picture has a corner cut off for uniformity).

3. Use the brush to spread a light layer of the tapioca mixture at the top of the wrapper.

4. Place a reasonable amount of the stuffing on the lower center of the wrapper.

5. Once you have the stuffing exactly where you want it (you can shape it a little with your hands), take the bottom corner...

6. and bring it up and over the stuffing - tuck the wrapper tightly under the mix.

44

HOW TO MAKE SPRING ROLLS - part 2

7. Roll it tight and stop about half way.

8. At this point take the corners in and bring them to center.

9. The side flaps will likely overlap.

10. Continue to wrap firmly.

11. Secure the flap by gently pressing (the tapioca mixture works like glue)

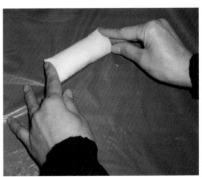

12. And here is a beautiful spring roll ready to fry!

LARB GAI

A recipe adapted from Laotian cuisine. It is a festive dish for religious and wedding celebrations. It is one of my customers' favorite appetizers. It can also be served as a main course with sticky rice or steamed rice .

4 servings

Ingredients:
½ pound ground chicken breast
2 tablespoons fresh lime juice (or to taste)
1 tablespoon fish sauce (or to taste)
1 tablespoon fresh ground lemon grass
1 tablespoon Roasted Ground Rice (page 17)
¼ cup chopped cilantro (or more, according to your taste)
¼ cup chopped green onion
1 teaspoon ground hot chili pepper (add more, if you like it hotter)
2 tablespoons Emerald Stir-Frying Sauce (page 134)
lettuce leaves
cooking oil

Method:
1. Cook ground chicken in a frying pan with a little oil. Stir until the chicken is almost done. Add the Emerald sauce. Stir until the chicken is cooked. Remove from heat.
2. In a mixing bowl, mix the chicken mixture with lime juice, fish sauce, and ground lemon grass, chili pepper, and roasted ground rice. Taste for flavor.
3. Add green onion and cilantro. Mix well. Transfer to serving plate.
4. Serve with lettuce leaves, by wrapping a spoonful of meat mixture in a piece of lettuce.

Note: If you do not like cilantro, you can substitute shredded mint leaves.

EMERALD BUTTERFLIES

Crab Rangoon, a well-known appetizer in Polynesian cuisine, with my own seasoning concept. It has been the most requested appetizer at the Emerald of Siam.

40 Butterflies

Ingredients:
1 pound cream cheese
1 pound medium thick wonton wrappers (about 40 sheets)
1 tablespoon light soy sauce or Thai soy sauce
½ cup imitation crab meat, chopped into small pieces with a food processor
¼ cup chopped green onion
vegetable oil for deep frying

Method:
1. In a large mixing bowl, mix cream cheese, soy sauce, crab meat, and green onion. Mix well. Refrigerate the mixture for at least 1 hour.
2. To make each butterfly, spoon about 1 teaspoon of cream cheese in the middle of each wonton wrapper. Make 1 at a time. *(See illustration on next page.)* Use warm water on your finger to draw a diamond on the wonton wrapper. Fold the opposite sides, pinch sides where the water lines meet. The edges will open to look like butterfly wings.
3. Deep-fry butterflies in hot oil (325-350 degrees) until golden brown.
4. Remove from oil with a strainer. Rest the butterflies on a platter lined with paper towels to blot out excess oil. Serve hot with Sweet and Sour Sauce (page 135).

HOW TO MAKE BUTTERFLIES - part 1

1. Set out ingredients to make Butterflies. Wonton wrappers, cream cheese, hot water, and a spoon.

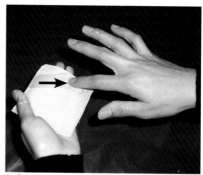

2. Dip your finger in hot water and draw a diamond in the wrapper as shown.

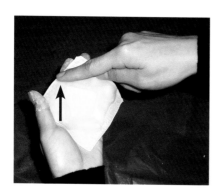

3. Use the spoon or your fingers to place a ball of cream cheese mixture in the center of the wonton wrap.

50

HOW TO MAKE BUTTERFLIES - part 2

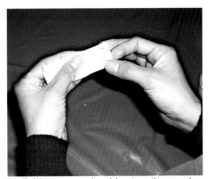

4. Fold two opposite sides together - only where Nok's left thumb is should be where the paper contacts and seals.

5. Pull up the middle of the other side to meet the crease. Apply light pressure to seal there.

This is another view.

6. Pinch up the other side into the middle and lightly pinch the wrapper that surrounds the ball of cream cheese.

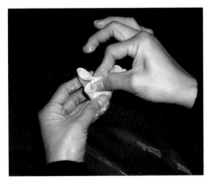

Be gentle!

A beautiful butterfly with wings!

SPICY FISH-CAKES

A unique appetizer very popular with the Thai people. It is served in most Thai restaurants and sold in Thai markets for consumers to take home for family dinner. In Thailand, we use a certain kind of white fish which has a very firm texture for this recipe. Since I could not find this fish, I decided to be creative by adding chicken breast to help with the texture. It turned out to be just right.

2 dozen Fish-Cakes

Ingredients:
½ pound fillet white fish, cut into small pieces (Note: I found that tilapia fillet is a good choice for this recipe.)
½ pound boneless and skinless chicken breast, cut into small pieces
2 large eggs
2 tablespoons red curry paste
½ tablespoon sugar
1 tablespoon fish sauce
¼ cup shredded fresh kaffir lime leaves
½ pound fresh green beans, cut into small pieces
vegetable oil for deep-frying

Method:
1. Mix fish, chicken, eggs, curry paste, sugar, and fish sauce in a mixing bowl.
2. Transfer the mixture to a food processor. Using the high-speed setting, process until the mixture becomes a paste.
3. Add kaffir lime leaves. Process for another 30 seconds. Put the paste back into the mixing bowl. Add green beans. Mix well with the paste.
4. Dampen your hands with cold water. Make the paste into a small ball and then press into a mini-pancake, before dropping into the hot oil.
5. Heat the oil to about 350-370 degrees. Drop in 1 cake at a time until the surface of the oil is covered. Turn the cakes over several times until they are cooked and brown.
6. Remove the fish-cakes with a strainer and place on a plate lined with paper towels.
7. Follow the same procedure for each fish-cake.
8. Serve with Cucumber Salad (page 133), topped with ground peanuts.

CHICKEN SATAY WITH PEANUT SAUCE

Another popular appetizer, served in Thai restaurants. When I was a child, we used to buy the Satay from one particular vendor, who was famous and well-known. When we were done eating, the waiter would come and count the skewers, to see how many we had consumed.

2 dozen

Ingredients:
2   boneless chicken breasts, cut into thin strips
2   dozen 8-inch bamboo skewers, soaked in water for about 30 minutes
    before use
1   can (13.5 oz.) coconut milk (save 1/4 cup for basting)
1   tablespoon curry powder
1   stalk fresh lemon grass (dice only the white part) or 1 tablespoon frozen
    ground lemon grass (now available in most Asian stores)
1   tablespoon fish sauce   1-2 tablespoons red curry paste
4   kaffir lime leaves   1-2 tablespoons tamarind juice
1/3 cup + 1 teaspoon sugar   1   teaspoon salt
½   cup creamy peanut butter   2   tablespoons vegetable oil
3/4 cup water

Method:
1. Marinate chicken strips for at least 1 hour with 2 tablespoons coconut milk, 1 teaspoon sugar, lemon grass, fish sauce, kaffir lime leaves, and curry powder.
2. Thread meat onto bamboo skewers. Keep refrigerated until ready to grill.
3. Prepare peanut sauce: heat oil over medium-low heat in a saucepan or wok. Add curry paste and sauté until you can detect the aroma of the curry. Add the water, the rest of coconut milk, and peanut butter. Stir and cook until the mixtures are well-blended over medium-high heat. When the oil starts to appear on the surface, add sugar, salt, and tamarind juice. Keep stirring until the sauce comes to a boil. Keep stirring for another 5 minutes. Remove from heat. Transfer to a serving dish.
4. Grill the chicken over charcoal grill or an open skillet. Baste meat during cooking with the rest of the coconut milk, using a small basting brush. Turn meat over a few times or until meat looks brown and cooked. Serve hot with Peanut Sauce (page 133) and Cucumber Salad (page 33).

CRISPY YUM-YUMS

An addictive appetizer named by my son Billy. It is easy to prepare. A good choice to bring to a baby shower, to work, or to share with co-workers.

160 pieces

Ingredients:
1 pack medium (thickness) wonton wrappers
1 cup sugar
1 cup water
1 teaspoon salt
¼ chopped green onions
    vegetable oil for deep frying

Method:
1. Cut the wonton wrappers diagonally into 4 sections. Separate them.
2. In a large deep-frying pan, heat the oil to 350 degrees.
3. Add wontons 1 at a time to see if the oil is ready, then add a handful at a time. The wontons should spring up immediately. If they do not do that, it shows that the oil is not hot enough. When the wontons turn golden brown and crispy, transfer them to a strainer first, then to a large mixing bowl. Set aside.
4. In a small saucepan, add water, sugar, and salt. Mix well. Over high heat, bring the mixture to a boil. Lower heat to medium-high. Cook until the mixture is syrupy. Add the green onions. Pour the syrup over the fried wontons. Toss the wontons with 2 long utensils until well-coated.
5. Transfer the Crispy Yum-Yums to the serving tray. For Christmas parties, you may want to sprinkle some red and green sprinkles on top to make it look festive.

EMERALD CHICKEN WINGS

Another popular item from the Emerald of Siam's lunch buffet menu.
A good appetizer to take to a football party.

48 pieces

Ingredients:
2 dozen chicken wings
1 tablespoon chopped garlic
1 tablespoon chopped cilantro root
1 tablespoon chopped lemon grass (available frozen in Asian markets)
3 tablespoons Thai soy sauce
1 tablespoon sugar
1 teaspoon salt
2 teaspoons black pepper
  oil for deep frying

Method:
1. Cut the joints of the chicken wings. Discard the wing tips. Put wings in a large mixing bowl and set aside.
2. Chop together the garlic, cilantro root, and lemon grass until fine and well-blended. Mix the chopped ingredients with Thai soy sauce, salt, sugar, and black pepper. Add sauce mixture to the chicken wings. Marinate the wings overnight or at least 12 hours before cooking.
3. Heat oil in frying pan to 400 degrees. Remove chicken wings from marinade and deep-fry in heated oil until wings turn golden brown, or meat is cooked.
4. Serve hot with steamed rice or serve cold as an appetizer.

To Mom With Love

I thought I had learned.

I was mistaken:

She is not my mother.
The Earth is my mother.

I was mistaken:

She isn't my teacher.
Life is my teacher.

I am the new learner:

She is my angel.

-Billy Quinn
Mother's Day, 1996

VEGETARIAN MENU

When I published "Joy of Thai Cooking" 17 years ago, I was not aware that there were many vegetarians in the community where I lived. We decided to have also a vegetarian menu for those patrons. The word got out. Now we see more vegetarians than we did before, and we are happy to serve their special needs. Thai spices make vegetables more joyful to eat. In the following recipes, you can substitute water for chicken broth, and light soy sauce for fish sauce.

Vegetable Lemon Grass Soup

Sunshine Rolls

Vegetarian Spring Rolls

Garlic Tofu Over Vegetables

Stir-Fried Emerald Vegetables

Asparagus With Black Mushrooms

Pahd Thai Vegetarian Style

Green Curry With Tofu

Bathing Rama Vegetarian Style

Larb Tofu

VEGETABLE LEMON GRASS SOUP

Looking for flavor in vegetables, the soup for you. It is also a good remedy for the common cold.

4 servings

Ingredients:
2 cups of a variety of cut-up vegetables (choose your favorite ones)
2 tablespoons sour chili paste (check label, it says there is no shrimp)
2 tablespoons fresh lime juice
1 tablespoon fish sauce (soy sauce for vegans)
1 stalk lemon grass, cut into slices
4 fresh kaffir lime leaves
1 medium tomato, cut into 6 wedges
5 cups chicken stock (water for vegans)
1 chunk galangal, cut into 1/8-inch-thick slices
3 fresh hot chili peppers (optional)
¼ cup chopped cilantro

Method:
1. Bring chicken stock to a boil.
2. Add kaffir lime leaves, lemon grass, and galangal. Boil for about 3 minutes. Add all vegetables, including tomato.
3. Mix sour chili paste, lime juice, and fish sauce into a small bowl. Add the mixture to the boiling broth with vegetables.
4. Return the mixture to a boil. Boil for 2 more minutes.
5. Taste the mixture for flavor. Add chili pepper, if you like it very spicy. Garnish with cilantro. Serve hot.

SUNSHINE ROLLS

Vietnamese-style fresh rolls - very well-liked by health-conscious consumers. They are very beautiful to look at, as well as flavorful, and make healthy appetizers. They can satisfy your appetite without a main course. Vegetarians love them.

1 dozen

Ingredients:
12 rice paper wrappers
12 green lettuce leaves (only the green part)
1 cup shredded carrot
1 large de-seeded cucumbers, cut into 2"x¼" strips
2 cups cooked and cooled rice noodles (medium- or small-width)
1½ cup fried tofu, cut into strips
1 cup chopped cilantro

Method:
1. Use a large shallow bowl filled ¾ of the way with the hottest water from your tap.
2. One at a time, making sure that water covers the entire sheet, dip the dry wrappers into the water for 6 seconds.
3. Remove the sheet from the water carefully, allowing for excess water to drip back into the bowl, and place the wrapper flat on a clean dry surface (not wood - it will stick).
4. Place 1 lettuce leaf, a generous pinch of carrots, a few strips of fried tofu, a few strips of cucumber, a pinch of cilantro, and a pinch of rice noodles on the center of the rice paper.
5. Roll like a tight burrito *(see illustration on next page)*.
6. Serve with Peanut Sauce (page 133), or Emerald House Dressing (page 135). You also can serve with your favorite lo-cal dressing.

Note: Sunshine Rolls should be served within 24 hours. Keep covered until serving time.

HOW TO MAKE SUNSHINE ROLLS - part 1

1. Fully submerge the rice paper into the hot water. (We use an electric wok at 250 degrees)

2. Remove from water - allow excess water to drip off before setting on clean surface. Arrange the lettuce flat in the center.

3. Spread the shredded carrots evenly on the lettuce.

4. Follow with cucumber slices.

5. Add tofu strips and cilantro.

6. Add rice noodles.

HOW TO MAKE SUNSHINE ROLLS - part 2

7. Bring bottom edge of rice paper over the top (keep tight).

8. Roll the vegetables with rice paper tight to the center.

9. Bring the sides of rice paper to the middle.

10. Tightly roll up the bundle to the top of the rice paper.

11. Keep rolling until the edge is sealed.

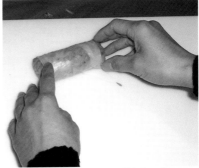

12. Here you have a beautiful Sunshine Roll.

VEGETARIAN SPRING ROLLS

A recipe inspired by all the beauty of all the colors of different all the fresh vegetables. They should be welcomed by the human body. When these vegetables are stir-fried together, with the help of a little salt and white ground pepper, the natural sweet taste of the onion and cabbage makes this appetizer most enjoyable for vegetarians and non-vegetarians, alike.

2 dozen

Ingredients:
2 cups prepared bean threads, cut into 3-inch sections
¼ cup shredded wood-ear mushrooms, soaked in cold water
2 tablespoons tapioca starch mixed with 1 cup hot water to form a paste to seal the spring rolls

1 pound fresh bean sprouts	1 head small cabbage, shredded
1 cup chopped onion	½ cup shredded carrot
½ cup frozen green peas	½ tablespoon chopped garlic
1 teaspoon salt	1 teaspoon white ground pepper
2 dozen spring roll wrappers	2 tablespoons vegetable oil
oil for deep frying	

Method:
1. Blanch cabbage and bean sprouts separately in boiling water. Blanch the cabbage first. Remove it from the hot water to a strainer as soon as the cabbage changes its color to bright green. When water returns to a boil, add bean sprouts. Remove the bean sprouts after 1 minute and transfer to the strainer with the cabbage.
2. Sauté garlic in heated oil over medium-high heat until it turns golden brown.
3. Add onion, carrot, green peas, and mushrooms. Stir-fry for 2 minutes.
4. Add cabbage, bean sprouts, and bean threads. Stir-fry for 2 minutes.
5. Add salt and white ground pepper. Stir-fry for 2 more minutes.
6. Remove the mixture to a strainer. Use a large tray lined with several layers of paper towels. Transfer the mixture to the tray. Spread out the mixture evenly to cool down. Store in the refrigerator until it is completely cooled before making into spring rolls.
7. To make Thai Spring Rolls, see illustrations on pages 44 and 45.

GARLIC TOFU OVER VEGETABLES

A dish always requested by our vegetarian customers and by my son Bill whenever he does not want any meat in his food.

4 servings

Ingredients:
½ pound fried tofu, cut into bite-size cubes
2 tablespoons Emerald Stir-Frying Sauce (page 134)
½ tablespoon granulated garlic
1 teaspoon ground black or white pepper
1 tablespoon fried garlic
3 tablespoons vegetable oil

Method:
1. Marinate all ingredients, except the vegetable oil and the fried garlic, for about 10 minutes, while you prepare the stir-fried vegetables.
2. Prepare the Stir-Fried Emerald Vegetables (page 73).
3. Heat the oil over high heat, add the marinated tofu, and stir-fry for a few minutes or until the tofu looks crisp on the outside.
4. Remove the tofu to a strainer to get rid of the excess oil.
5. Mix the fried garlic with the tofu and spread the tofu over the prepared Stir-Fried Emerald Vegetables. Serve hot over steamed rice.

STIR-FRIED EMERALD VEGETABLES

One of my joys in the kitchen at the Emerald preparing all the fresh vegetables for the day. This dish is always on the buffet table to make sure that my customers have the vegetables they need for the day.

4 servings

Ingredients:
2 pounds assorted cut-up fresh vegetables: broccoli, green cabbage, fresh mushrooms, carrots, snow peas, baby corn, and zucchini
1 teaspoon chopped garlic
1 cup chicken broth
2 tablespoons Emerald Stir-Frying Sauce (page 134)
¼ teaspoon white ground pepper
2 tablespoons vegetable oil

Method:
1. Heat the chicken broth in a large saucepan or wok. Bring to a boil.
2. Add fresh vegetables to the boiling broth. Stir and mix thoroughly. As soon as the broccoli and the snow peas change their color to bright green, remove them and the excess broth to a large bowl. Set aside.
3. Heat vegetable oil in the same cooking pan, over high heat. Add garlic and vegetables (including liquid) and Emerald Stir-Frying Sauce. Sprinkle with white pepper. Stir and mix one more time.
4. Transfer the vegetables to a serving platter. Serve hot, over steamed rice.

ASPARAGUS WITH BLACK MUSHROOMS

Beautiful locally-grown asparagus --- never to be ignored during the Spring. It is bountiful for two months a year. I always serve this dish on the lunch or dinner buffet at my restaurant, with or without meat.

4 servings

Ingredients:
1½ pounds of fresh asparagus (discard the hard part), soaked in cold water
½ cup black mushrooms, soaked 30 minutes or more in a cup until soft
  (remove mushrooms and discard water)
4 cloves fresh garlic, crushed
3 tablespoons Emerald Stir-Frying Sauce (page 134)
½ cup chicken broth
1 cup fresh Thai basil leaves
¼ teaspoon white ground pepper
2 tablespoons cooking oil
8 cups boiling water

Method:
1. Rinse the asparagus well and cut into 3-inch sections.
2. Blanch the fresh asparagus in hot boiling water for 1 minute.
3. Remove from heat. Transfer the asparagus to a strainer. Put it aside.
4. In a frying pan, or wok, heat the oil over high heat. Add garlic and sauté until it turns light brown.
5. Add asparagus, black mushrooms, Emerald Stir-Frying Sauce, chicken broth, and white ground pepper. Stir-fry until the asparagus appears tender. Add Thai basil leaves. Stir-fry for 1 more minute. Remove from heat.
6. Transfer to a serving platter. Serve over steamed rice.

PAHD THAI VEGETARIAN STYLE

Every Thai cook's challenge --- this well-known Thai noodle dish. Pahd means stir-fry. Pahd Thai means stir-fry the Thai way. It is not a dish to be cooked at home. People in Thailand go to their favorite vendor to buy and take home this meal for their family.

4 servings

Ingredients:

½ pound Pahd Thai rice noodles
½ cup chopped onion
2 tablespoons chopped preserved turnip
½ cup fried tofu strips
1 cup fresh bean sprouts
3 green onions, cut into 1½ -inch sections
1 teaspoon hot chili pepper powder (optional)
4 tablespoons Tamarind Flavored Sauce (page 136) or to taste

1 egg, beaten
1 teaspoon chopped garlic
2 tablespoons vegetable oil
½ tablespoon fish sauce
1/3 cup ground peanuts
1 teaspoon ground paprika
1 fresh lime, quartered

Method:

1. Soak dry rice noodles in cold water for 1 hour before cooking. Drain. Put noodles aside.
2. Heat oil in a non-stick cooking pan over medium-high heat. Add garlic, onion, preserved turnip, and fried tofu. Stir-fry for 2 minutes.
3. Add Tamarind Flavored Sauce, fish sauce, and paprika.
4. Increase heat to high. Add noodles. Stir and cook until the noodles mix well with the sauce and become soft (if the noodles remain dry, add some water, as needed, to soften them).
5. Add peanuts, bean sprouts, and green onions. Stir and cook until the vegetables are well-heated.
6. Make a well in the middle of the mixture. Put in the egg. Cover the egg with the noodle mixture for 1 minute. Stir and mix well until the egg is done. Remove from heat. Transfer the Pahd Thai to a serving platter. Garnish with fresh bean sprouts, lime wedge, and hot chili powder.

GREEN CURRY WITH TOFU

My favorite of all curries. In Thailand, we use baby Thai eggplant for this dish. Bamboo shoot strips are a good substitute. It is also a favorite among vegetarians. The green curry truly enhances both the presentation and the flavor of the vegetables in this dish.

4 servings

Ingredients:
½ pound fresh firm tofu or fried tofu (available in health food stores)
1 can (13.5 oz.) coconut milk (unsweetened)
1 can (8 oz.) bamboo shoot strips or 1 cup cut-up vegetables of
of your choice
2 tablespoons green curry paste
2 tablespoons vegetable oil
4 fresh kaffir lime leaves
2 teaspoons sugar
2 tablespoons fish sauce
½ cup fresh Thai basil leaves
½ cup sliced green bell pepper
2 fresh chili peppers (optional)

Method:
1. Sauté curry paste in oil over low heat until it becomes aromatic. (High heat will burn the curry paste.)
2. Spoon the thick and creamy part of the coconut milk from the can. Add to the curry. Increase the heat. Stir and mix well. Cook until the coconut cream blends well with the curry.
3. Add kaffir lime leaves, bamboo shoots, and the rest of the coconut milk. Stir and cook until the mixture comes to a boil.
4. Add tofu, green pepper, and Thai basil leaves. Cook to a boil again. Add fish sauce and sugar to your taste. If you want extra spicy, add the fresh chili pepper 1 minute before removing the curry from the heat.
5. Serve with steamed rice.

BATHING RAMA VEGETARIAN STYLE

This curry dish, with a fancy name --- cooking contest winner in the '60s. I did not know anything about cooking then. The original dish was prepared with beef and Chinese watercress. Broccoli and spinach are very good substitutes.

4 servings

Ingredients:
½ pound fresh firm tofu or fried tofu, cut into bite-sized pieces
1 bunch fresh spinach (cleaned well)
½ cup Peanut Sauce (page 133)

Method:
1. Heat the tofu in the microwave for 2 minutes.
2. Blanch the spinach in hot boiling water. Remove with a strainer to a serving platter. Spread it evenly to cover the plate.
3. Put the heated tofu evenly on top of the spinach, followed with the Peanut Sauce.

Note: The fried tofu will look more appealing if deep-fried before being cut into small pieces instead of being reheated in the microwave.

LARB TOFU

A flavorful appetizer for vegetarians. The fried tofu can be purchased in any Asian store or health food store. Choose the kind with texture that can absorb liquid better.

4 servings

Ingredients:
12 oz. fried tofu, cut into small cubes
1 tablespoon Emerald Stir-Frying Sauce (page 134)
1 tablespoon fish sauce
3 tablespoons fresh lime juice
2 tablespoons Roasted Ground Rice (page 17)
1 teaspoon chili power
¼ cup chopped cilantro
¼ cup chopped green onion
1 tablespoon ground fresh lemon grass (now available frozen in Asian markets)

Method:
1. Sauté tofu in sauce pan with Emerald Stir-Frying Sauce until the sauce is well-mixed with tofu and heated throughout.
2. Remove from heat. Transfer the mixture to a mixing bowl.
3. Add lime juice, fish sauce, chili powder, lemon grass, and Roasted Ground Rice.
4. Adjust the mixture to your taste, add fish sauce or lime juice as needed. Add green onion and cilantro. Transfer to a serving plate. Serve with lettuce.

When I Kiss A Rose

When I kiss a Rose
I kiss myself.

When I love a child
I love myself.

When I hold a friend
I hold myself.

When I hold an enemy
God holds me.

-Alima Ravadi Quinn

The Masters

When I read the Scripture
I found unconditional love on the Cross.

When I read Buddha's teachings
I found the power of the mind.

When I read Rumi's poems
I found myself swimming in the ocean of love.

-Alima Ravadi Quinn

CURRIES

Green Chicken Curry (Gaeng Kiaw Wan Gai)

Indian Style Curry

Tropical Shrimp Curry

Pork Curry With Pineapple

Massamun Beef Curry

Chicken Panang Curry

GREEN CHICKEN CURRY (Gaeng Kiaw Wan Gai)

One of the most popular curries among the Thai. It is served in all Thai restaurants in the USA. The bamboo shoots are a substitute for baby eggplant which is rare to find in USA markets.

4 servings

Ingredients:
1 pound boneless chicken breast, cut into small strips
1 can (13.5 oz.) coconut milk
1 can (8 oz.) bamboo shoot strips
2 tablespoons green curry paste
2 tablespoons vegetable oil
4 fresh or dried kaffir lime leaves
2 teaspoons sugar
2 tablespoons fish sauce
1 cup fresh Thai basil leaves (available all-year-round in Asian markets)
1 small green pepper, sliced
2 fresh hot chili peppers (optional)

Method:
1. Sauté curry paste in oil on low heat until curry becomes aromatic. (High heat will burn the curry paste.)
2. Spoon the thick and creamy part of the coconut milk from the can and add to the curry. Increase heat. Stir and mix well; cook until the coconut milk blends well with the curry (about 3 minutes).
3. Add chicken. Increase heat to high. Stir and cook until the chicken is almost done.
4. Add kaffir lime leaves, bamboo shoots, and the rest of the coconut milk. Bring the mixture to a boil. Stir and mix well. Cook until the chicken is done (no longer pink).
5. Add fish sauce and sugar, to taste. Add green pepper, basil leaves, and hot chili pepper. Return the mixture to a boil.
6. Remove from heat. Serve over steamed rice.

INDIAN STYLE CURRY

"Carries" a taste of exotic Thailand. The yellow curry paste, however, has mostly Indian spices. Vegetarians will love this dish with fresh or fried tofu.

4 servings

Ingredients:

1 pound boneless chicken breast, cut into 1½-inch strips, or
   ½ pound tofu of your choice, cut into 2/3-inch cubes
2-3 tablespoons yellow curry paste
1 can (13.5 oz.) coconut milk
1-2 tablespoons fish sauce, or to taste
1 teaspoon sugar
4 kaffir lime leaves
2 small cooked potatoes, peeled and quartered
2 tablespoons vegetable oil

Method:

1. Sauté curry paste in heated oil over medium heat.
2. Add the thick part of the coconut milk from the can, and the kaffir lime leaves. Stir and cook until the curry and coconut milk are well-blended (when the oil starts to appear on the surface).
3. Add chicken or the tofu of your choice, and the rest of the coconut milk.
4. Increase heat to high. Bring the mixture to a boil. Stir and cook until the meat is done (if you use chicken).
5. Add potatoes, fish sauce, and sugar.
6. Bring the mixture to a boil. Stir and cook for 2 more minutes. Then, remove from heat.
7. Serve over steamed rice.

TROPICAL SHRIMP CURRY

A good dish for seafood lovers. It is "pleasing to the eye" as well as to the stomach. The pineapple will take you to the warm country when you prepare this dish in winter.

4 servings

Ingredients:
½ pound large shrimp (12-16 count)
2 tablespoons red curry paste
1 can (13.5 oz.) coconut milk
1 can (8 oz.) pineapple chunks (discard the juice)
4 fresh lime leaves
½ cup fresh Thai basil leaves
1 tablespoon fish sauce
½ tablespoon sugar
½ sliced green bell pepper
2 tablespoons vegetable oil

Method:
1. Shell and de-vein the shrimp. Set aside.
2. Heat vegetable oil in a saucepan or wok over low heat. Add curry paste, sauté until you can detect the aroma of the curry.
3. Spoon the thick and creamy part of the coconut milk from the can and add to the curry. Increase heat to medium-high. Keep stirring until the curry paste and coconut milk are well-blended (mixture will appear red).
4. Add kaffir lime leaves, pineapple, and the rest of the coconut milk. Stir until the mixture comes to a boil. Keep cooking for 2 more minutes.
5. Add shrimp, basil leaves, and bell pepper. Cook until the shrimp turn pink. Add fish sauce and sugar, to taste. Boil for 1 more minute. Remove from heat. Serve with steamed rice.

Note: If you desire a more spicy curry, add Thai Hot Sauce (page 132) to enhance the flavors.

PORK CURRY WITH PINEAPPLE

A popular curry at the Emerald on Wednesday's buffet. I was asked to include this recipe in the book. If you are vegetarian, you can replace the pork with fresh or fried tofu.

4 servings

Ingredients:
½ pound boneless lean pork loin, cut into 1½ inch by 1-inch strips
1-2 tablespoons red curry paste
1 can (13.5 oz.) coconut milk
4 fresh kaffir lime leaves
1 tablespoon fish sauce
2 teaspoons sugar
1 small green pepper, cut into strips
2 tablespoons vegetable oil
1 can (8 oz.) pineapple tidbits, drained, or 1 cup of fresh pineapple bits

Method:
1. Sauté curry paste in heated oil over low heat. Stir and mix well until you can detect the aroma of the curry paste. Put aside.
2. Scoop the thick, creamy part of the coconut milk from the can and add it to the curry mixture. Increase heat to medium-high. Stir and cook for a few minutes, or until you can see the oil start to appear on the surface.
3. Add kaffir lime leaves, pork strips, and the rest of the coconut milk.
4. Increase heat to high. Bring the mixture to a boil. Cook until the meat is done. Add pineapple and green pepper. Bring the mixture to a boil again. Stir and cook for 2 minutes.
5. Add fish sauce and sugar to taste. Remove from heat. Serve over rice.

MASSAMUN BEEF CURRY

Also known as Massamun, Matsuman, Mussaman - you name it. I learned this dish from a Muslim friend from Thailand. It has been a very popular item on the Emerald dinner buffet, once a month. The preparation is a little different from my first cookbook, "Joy of Thai Cooking." It takes time to cook, but it is well worthwhile.

8 servings

Ingredients:
2½ pounds boneless beef roast, cut into 1½-inch cubes
2 cans (13.5 oz.) coconut milk
1 can water (13.5 oz.)
1 large onion, cut into 6 sections
4 red potatoes, peeled and quartered
4 tablespoons Massamun curry paste
¼ cup sugar
2 tablespoons tamarind juice
1 teaspoon salt
¼ cup + 2 tablespoons vegetable oil
½ cup roasted peanut (optional)

Method:
1. In a large saucepan, add the coconut milk and water. Set aside.
2. In a skillet, heat up the vegetable oil with high heat. Cook the beef until no longer red. Add the curry paste and onion. Stir-fry until well-mixed. Set aside.
3. Heat up the coconut milk over high heat until it comes to a boil. Add the meat mixture. Keep cooking until the meat is tender. Stir the mixture frequently while cooking. Add sugar, tamarind juice (see note below), and salt. Stir the mixture and cook until the sugar is well-dissolved. Add potatoes and cook until the potatoes are tender.
4. Remove from heat. Serve hot with steamed rice.

Note: Add 1 tablespoon of tamarind juice first, then taste for the balance between sugar and salt.

95

CHICKEN PANANG CURRY

Still one of my son Billy's favorite dishes. He always used to order this curry dish when he was a teenager. Back then, there were only a few dishes at the Emerald that would satisfy his appetite.

4 servings

Ingredients:
1 pound boneless, skinless chicken breast, cut into bite-sized pieces
1 can (13.5 oz) unsweetened coconut milk
2 tablespoons panang curry paste
6 fresh kaffir lime leaves, cut into small strips
1 tablespoon fish sauce
1 teaspoon sugar
1 small green or red bell pepper, cut into small strips
½ cup or more fresh Thai basil leaves
2 tablespoons cooking oil

Method:
1. Sauté curry paste in heated oil over low heat. Stir the mixture well until you can detect the aroma of the curry paste.
2. Scoop the thick, creamy part of the coconut milk from the can and add it to the curry mix. Increase heat to medium-high. Stir and cook for a few minutes, or until the oil starts to appear on the surface.
3. Add chicken meat and kaffir lime leaves. Increase heat to high. Stir and cook until the meat is done. Add the rest of the coconut milk.
4. Continue cooking until the mixture comes to a boil. Add the bell pepper, fish sauce, sugar, and basil leaves. Taste for flavor until the balance satisfies your palate. Be careful - it's hot!
5. Remove from heat. Serve over steamed rice.

Note: If you like it spicier, stir in a few strips of hot chili pepper before removing from the heat. Thai Hot Sauce (page 132) also works well if you would rather use that instead of chili peppers.

Haiku

God waits to be born.
Only one thing blocks the way,
And it bears my name.

10/24/94

On the trillionth day,
God said, I'm having fun now!
And the game went on.

12/22/94

Inner life is NOT
What goes on inside your head.
Dig a foot deeper!

03/13/95

And so I led her
To the edge of the ocean.
And she drank it up!

10/08/96

Do not throw yourself
At the feet of your teacher.
Leave, and live his word!

06/03/97

I love things that change--
Butterflies and frogs-- but most,
What I shall become!

08/19/97

-Alim Quinn

MAIN DISHES

Thai Style Sweet And Sour Pork (Moo Priew Wahn)

Plah Rahd Prik

Drunken Chicken (Pahd Kee-Mao Gai)

Spicy Shrimp Fried Rice

Cashew Chicken

Son-In-Law's Eggs

Thai Omelette

Chicken With Bean Threads (Pahd Woon Sen)

Pahd See-Iw

Smoked Salmon Fried Rice

Garlic Shrimp (Goong Tod Gratiam Prik Thai)

Garlic Pork

Spicy Garlic Chicken (Gratiam Prik Thai Gai)

Thai Roast Duck

Chicken With Ginger (Gai Pahd King)

THAI STYLE SWEET AND SOUR PORK
(Moo Priew Wahn)

A dish that has surprised some new customers at the Emerald (when the waiter forgot to inform them that the meat was not breaded like the Chinese version).

4 servings

Ingredients:
1 pound pork loin, cut into strips and marinated with 1 tablespoon sesame oil and 1 tablespoon cornstarch
1 small onion, cut into 8 sections
1 small tomato, cut into 8 sections
1 small green pepper, cut into 8 sections
1 small cucumber, seeded and cut into sections
1 can (8 oz.) pineapple chunks, drained
3 tablespoons tomato ketchup
1 tablespoon chopped fresh garlic
2 tablespoons vegetable oil

Make this sauce and set aside:
2 tablespoons Emerald Stir-Frying Sauce (page 134) with ½ cup Tamarind Flavored Sauce (page 136)

Method:
1. Cook garlic in heated oil at medium heat until golden brown.
2. Add pork mixture, increase heat to high. Stir and cook until pork is no longer pink.
3. Add sauce mixture. Cook it to a boil.
4. Add prepared vegetables, pineapple, and tomato ketchup. Stir and cook, bringing to a boil. Continue cooking for 1 minute. If the sauce is dry, add some water. Taste for flavors.
5. Remove from heat. Serve over steamed rice.

PLAH RAHD PRIK

Not in favor of cooking fish in my kitchen. I regret to say I don't care for the fishy odor in my house. But I do love to eat fish - in Thailand these fish dishes are prepared outdoors. I am very happy to share this recipe with you. It is served in most Thai restaurants.

4 servings

Ingredients:
1   pound salmon or halibut fillet (if you cannot find any whole pomfret)
½ cup chopped onion
½ cup sliced green pepper
1/3 cup carrot strips
1/3 cup ginger strips (fresh or from a jar)
2   tablespoons Emerald Stir-Frying Sauce (page 134)
½ cup Tamarind Flavored Sauce (page 136)
½ cup Thai basil leaves
½ cup chopped cilantro
½ tablespoon chopped garlic
3   hot chili peppers, sliced (optional)
    vegetable oil for deep-frying

Method:
1. Deep-fry fish fillet until it is cooked. Remove from oil to a serving platter.
2. Leave only 2 tablespoons oil in the cooking pan.
3. With medium-high heat, add garlic and cook until light brown. Add everything else except cilantro. Stir-fry and cook until the mixture comes to a boil. Add hot chili pepper if you want it spicy. Stir and mix well. Remove from heat. Pour the sauce over the fried fish. Garnish with chopped cilantro.

Note: The original dish calls for whole white pomfret. It is available frozen in most Asian markets. If you decide to use whole fish, clean the fish well, and deep-fry until the whole fish is cooked and crispy.

DRUNKEN CHICKEN (Pahd Kee-Mao Gai)

A dish that always boosts up my energy with its extra spicy flavor. It is very inviting when you see the chicken mingling with the Thai basil, strips of fresh hot chili pepper, and slivers of kaffir lime leaves.

4 servings

Ingredients:
½ pound ground chicken breast (the Thais will chop the chicken with a large cleaver)
6 kaffir lime leaves, cut into strips
1 cup fresh Thai basil leaves
3 fresh hot chili peppers, cut in halves lengthwise
1 tablespoon Emerald Stir-Frying Sauce (page 134)
½ tablespoon fish sauce
1 teaspoon sugar
1 tablespoon chopped garlic
½ cup chicken broth
3 tablespoons vegetable oil

Method:
1. Heat the oil with medium heat.
2. Add garlic and stir-fry until the garlic turns light brown.
3. Add ground chicken and kaffir lime leaves. Increase heat to high.
4. Stir-fry until the chicken is almost done. Add chicken broth and Emerald Stir-Frying Sauce. Bring the mixture to a boil.
5. Add Thai basil and hot pepper. Stir and mix well. Cook for 1 more minute, adding fish sauce and sugar to taste.
6. Remove from heat and transfer the Drunken Chicken to a serving platter. Serve hot over steamed rice.

Note: Son-In-Law's Eggs (page 111) is a good complement to this dish.

SPICY SHRIMP FRIED RICE

A very flavorful dish when you cannot think of anything else. The colors of the shrimp and basil leaves are very "inviting to the eye," as well as to the stomach.

4 servings

Ingredients:
4 cups cooked rice
½ pound medium-sized raw shrimp
1 tablespoon chopped fresh garlic
½ cup chopped onion
3 fresh hot chili pepper (sliced in halves)
½ cup fresh mushrooms
½ cup sliced green pepper
3 tablespoons Emerald Stir-Frying Sauce (page 134)
1 tablespoon fish sauce
1-2 teaspoons sugar
½ cup fresh Thai basil leaves
1 large egg (beaten)
2 tablespoons vegetable oil

Method:
1. Shell and de-vein the shrimp. Set aside.
2. Heat the rice in a microwave for 1 minute if the rice is cold. Put aside.
3. In your wok or skillet, heat oil to medium heat. Sauté the garlic with vegetable oil until golden brown.
4. Add onion, green pepper, and fresh mushrooms. Stir-fry for 2 minutes.
5. Add shrimp, hot steamed rice, Emerald Stir-Frying Sauce, sugar, and fish sauce. Stir fry until the mixture is well-blended and the shrimp turn pink.
6. Add egg and stir-fry until the egg is cooked. Mix well.
7. Add basil leaves and hot chili pepper. Stir-fry for 1-2 minutes.
8. Remove from heat. Serve at once.

CASHEW CHICKEN

A recipe to choose out of several ways of preparing Cashew Chicken. I like the glamorous look of the chicken and the contrast of the dry chili pepper with its taste. I often take this dish to potluck parties.

4 servings

Ingredients:
1 pound boneless chicken breast with skin removed, cut into small strips
2 tablespoons minced garlic
2 teaspoons white ground pepper
4 tablespoons white or red wine
1 tablespoon corn starch
2 tablespoons Thai soy sauce
1 dozen dried chili peppers
½ cup whole raw cashew nuts
1/3 cup vegetable oil
1½ tablespoons black soy sauce

Method:
1. Marinate chicken meat with Thai soy sauce, garlic, ground pepper, wine, and corn starch for 30 minutes.
2. Heat oil over medium heat. Add cashew nuts and chili peppers. Stir-fry until cashew nuts turn golden. Remove both chili peppers and cashew nuts from oil with a strainer. Set aside.
3. Increase heat to high. Add marinated chicken. Stir and cook until the chicken is done. Add black soy sauce. Stir and mix well until all chicken meat is evenly coated and looks golden brown.
4. Add chili peppers and cashew nuts. Mix well and remove from heat. Transfer cashew chicken to a serving platter with a strainer to remove excess oil. Serve with steamed rice.

SON-IN-LAW'S EGGS

In Thailand known as "Kai luuk kuy." There is a story among the Thais about this well-known dish. A son-in-law was trying to impress his mother-in-law, who came to visit without warning. He came up with this idea on how to cook eggs with an interesting appearance, and with interesting flavor as well. In the original recipe, the eggs are boiled first, then shelled and deep-fried. I found it much easier and just as tasty to skip the boiling process. This recipe must have impressed the mother-in-law because the recipe has been passed on until this very day.

8 servings

Ingredients:
8 large eggs
½ cup Tamarind Flavored Sauce (page 136)
1 cup sliced onion
1 tablespoon fish sauce
½ cup chopped cilantro
  vegetable oil

Method:
1. Fry each egg so that only one side is crispy. Keep drizzling hot oil from pan on top of eggs to cook the yolk until almost fully cooked. Put the fried eggs on a serving platter, after using a strainer to drain off the oil.
2. In a frying pan, sauté the sliced onion in 2 tablespoons of vegetable oil over medium heat until it turns golden brown. Put aside.
3. In a small saucepan, mix the Tamarind Flavored Sauce with fish sauce. Cook it over medium-high heat and bring to a boil.
4. Add the sliced onion. Mix well.
5. Remove from heat and transfer to the serving platter. Spread the sauce over the fried eggs.
6. Garnish with chopped cilantro. Serve hot, with steamed rice.

Note: A good complement to any curry dish.

THAI OMELETTE

Was asked to include this recipe in this book. My daughter Dara always saves the leftovers for the next day's breakfast by making it into a breakfast burrito. Her little children enjoy it, too. You may want to try it sometime. Add some Salsa, too.

4 servings

Ingredients:
8 large eggs, beaten
2 tablespoons Emerald Stir-Frying Sauce (page 134)
½ teaspoon white ground pepper
1 cup sliced onion
½ cup sliced green pepper
½ sliced fresh mushroom
   vegetable oil

Method:
1. Mix all the ingredients, except the vegetable oil, in a large mixing bowl. Mix well.
2. In a skillet or wok, heat oil to medium-high heat.
3. Cook the mixture as you would cook a regular omelette, 1 small batch at a time until it is all gone, increasing heat as necessary.
4. Transfer each batch to a serving platter. Serve with steamed rice.

CHICKEN WITH BEAN THREADS (Pahd Woon Sen)

A popular, low-cal dish that complements any Thai curry dish that you might want for lunch or dinner.

8 servings

Ingredients:
8 oz. dried bean threads (comes in a package of 4 2-oz.-bundles)
½ pound boneless chicken breast, cut into bite-sized pieces
1 small yellow onion, sliced (about 1 cup)
3 green onions, cut into 1-inch lengths
6 eggs, beaten
1 tablespoon chopped garlic
1 teaspoon white ground pepper
½ cup Emerald Stir-Frying Sauce (page 134)
1 tablespoon sesame oil
4 tablespoons vegetable cooking oil

Method:
1. Soak in cold water until soft (about 30 minutes). Cut each bundle in half. Drain and put aside.
2. In a mixing bowl, combine bean threads, eggs, ground pepper, and Emerald Stir-Frying Sauce. Mix well. Put aside.
3. In a separate mixing bowl, marinate the chicken with sesame oil.
4. Heat 2 tablespoons of vegetable oil, over high heat in a non-stick skillet or wok.
5. Add garlic and chicken. Stir-fry until the chicken is done. Remove from heat. Put aside.
6. Heat the rest of the cooking oil over high heat in the same skillet or wok. Add the bean threads mixture. Stir-fry and cook until no liquid remains.
7. Stir in chicken and both kinds of onion. Stir-fry and cook for a few more minutes. Remove from heat. Transfer to a serving platter. Serve with steamed rice.

PAHD SEE-IW

Was asked to add this recipe to the cookbook. We added this dish to the menu recently, and it has been very popular ever since. It is great for lunch when you eat alone. You can add hot chili and Thai basil if you like your food spicy.

4 servings

Ingredients:
½ cup beef sirloin, cut into thin bite-sized pieces
½ tablespoon bean sauce
1 teaspoon chopped garlic (If you really like garlic, add more)
3 tablespoons Emerald Stir-Frying Sauce (page 134)
1 tablespoon fish sauce
1 teaspoon sugar
½ pound prepared rice noodles (wide width is best for this dish)
2 cups broccoli florets
2 tablespoons black soy sauce
¼ white ground pepper
1 teaspoon sesame oil
3 tablespoons vegetable oil
1 egg (optional)

Method:
1. Marinate meat with sesame oil and 1 tablespoon Emerald Stir-Frying Sauce. Put aside.
2. Blanch the broccoli florets with hot boiling water for 1 minute. Strain with a strainer. Put aside.
3. Prepare rice noodles according to instructions on the package.
4. In a non-stick frying pan, heat the oil over medium-high heat. Stir in garlic and bean sauce. Cook for 1 minute. Increase heat to high. Add meat and stir-fry until the meat is cooked.
5. Add noodles and black soy sauce. Stir-fry until the noodles are soft. Add broccoli, Emerald stir-frying sauce, fish sauce, sugar, and white pepper. Stir-fry the mixture until it is well-blended. Add egg and mix well until egg is cooked.
6. Remove from heat. Serve.

Note: If you want it spicy, stir in 1 cup fresh Thai basil leaves and a few sliced hot chili peppers 1 minute before removing from heat.

SMOKED SALMON FRIED RICE

Always fascinated by the "natural life" of Salmon of the Northwest. I was inspired to create this dish with pineapple, which is the famous fruit of that tropical land known as Thailand. The Thai basil enhances the aroma and the flavor of the rice, as well as dressing up its presentation when entertaining. A good potluck dish to serve at any party.

4 Servings

Ingredients:
4 cups cooked rice
½ pound smoked salmon, cut into bite sized pieces (discard the skin)
2 cups pineapple chunks (fresh or canned - drain if canned)
1 small green pepper, sliced (yields about 1 cup)
2 cups fresh Thai basil leaves
1 cup chopped onion
1/3 cup Emerald Stir-Frying Sauce (page 134)
4 cloves fresh garlic, crushed
4 tablespoons vegetable oil
4 fresh hot chili pepper, cut in halves lengthwise (optional)

Method:
1. Heat the rice in a microwave for 1 minute if the rice is cold. Put aside.
2. In a non-stick frying pan, heat the oil over medium heat. Add garlic and stir-fry until it turns light brown.
3. Add chopped onion, stir-fry for 1 minute. Add salmon, pineapple, and rice.
4. Increase heat to high. Stir-fry the mixture until thoroughly heated.
5. Add Emerald Stir-Frying Sauce, green pepper, and Thai basil. Keep stir-frying for a few minutes. (Add chili pepper if you desire this dish to be spicy. Stir for 1 more minute.) Remove from heat. Serve hot.

Note: Add more sauce if the flavor is not sufficiently robust.

GARLIC SHRIMP (Goong Tod Gratiam Prik Thai)

The fastest way to prepare a tasty dish of seafood. Served with stir-fried vegetables and steamed rice will make a happy meal.

4 servings

Ingredients:
1 pound large-sized shrimp (shelled and de-veined)
1 tablespoon granulated garlic
1 teaspoon white ground pepper
2 tablespoons Emerald Stir-Frying Sauce (page 134)
4 tablespoons vegetable oil
1 tablespoon fried garlic

Method:
1. Marinate shrimp with granulated garlic, white pepper, and Emerald Stir-Frying Sauce in a mixing bowl. Mix well. Set aside.
2. Heat oil with high heat until oil starts to smoke. Add shrimp mixture.
3. Stir and cook until the shrimp are cooked. Do not overcook. Remove from heat. Discard excess oil. Mix in fried garlic.
4. Transfer the garlic shrimp to a serving platter. Serve with steamed rice.

Note: You may prepare the same way with ½ pound beef strips if you would rather have red meat.

GARLIC PORK

Like to try a Thai breakfast? This dish, with some stir-fried vegetables, to accompany the boiled rice, is a healthy meal to start the day. If you do not like red meat, substitute chicken. If you are a vegetarian, substitute fried tofu instead of meat or chicken.

4 servings

Ingredients:
½ pound lean pork loin, cut into small strips
½ tablespoon granulated garlic
2 tablespoons Emerald Stir-Frying Sauce (page 134)
1 teaspoon ground black or white pepper
4 tablespoons vegetable oil

Method:
1. Marinate pork with all the ingredients (except for the vegetable oil) for about 10 minutes.
2. Heat oil over medium heat in a skillet or wok. When the oil gets very hot, add the meat mixture. Keep stirring until the meat is well-done and crunchy-looking. Remove from heat. Serve with boiled rice for breakfast, or with steamed rice for dinner.

Note: Boiled rice is very soothing for an unhappy stomach. Use 1 cup of cooked rice and 10 cups of water. Cook over high heat. Let it boil for a few minutes, or until the rice is soft. Remove from heat and serve warm.

SPICY GARLIC CHICKEN (Gratiam Prik Thai Gai)

Another comfort dish for me when I have low energy. I would have it very spicy. If you cannot take spice at all, leave out the hot pepper. It will taste just as good. It also tastes good the next day.

4 servings

Ingredients:
½ pound boneless chicken breast, cut into small strips
½ tablespoon granulated garlic (fresh garlic will burn before the chicken is done)
2 tablespoons Emerald Stir-Frying Sauce (page 134)
½ tablespoon ground white pepper
1-2 fresh hot chili peppers, chopped
4 tablespoons vegetable oil
2 tablespoons fried garlic

Method:
1. Marinate the chicken with granulated garlic, white pepper, and Emerald Stir-Frying Sauce. Set aside for 10 minutes.
2. Heat oil over high heat in a skillet or wok. When the oil gets very hot, add the chicken mixture. Keep stirring until the meat is well-done.
3. Stir in hot pepper and fried garlic. Mix well. Remove from heat.
4. Serve with steamed rice.

Note: Stir-Fried Emerald Vegetables (page 73) will give a good balance with this dish.

THAI ROAST DUCK

A recipe introduced to me by my youngest sister Sujitra. When I asked her for the recipe, she gave me the ingredients involved, without any portions or amounts. It took me a few trials to find the right recipe. I often serve this dish to my friends and family for Christmas.

4 servings

Ingredients:

1 5-6 pound duckling (not wild, please)
1½ cups chopped onion
1½ cups chopped parsley
1 teaspoon chopped garlic
1 tablespoon five-spice powder
3 teaspoons salt

1/3 cup + 2 tablespoons black soy sauce
2 tablespoons vegetable oil
½ cup honey mixed with
   ¼ cup white vinegar
¼ cup chopped cilantro for garnish

Method:

1. Preheat oven to 400 degrees.
2. Wash the duck and discard giblets. Rub the duck thoroughly with 2 teaspoons of salt. On a rack in a baking pan, with the breast side up, put the duck aside to let it air dry at room temperature.
3. To prepare for the stuffing: heat oil over medium-high heat. Add garlic and onion. Sauté for 2 minutes. Add five-spice powder and stir-fry for 2 more minutes. Add chopped parsley and sauté for 2 more minutes. Add soy sauce and water. Stir and cook over low heat for 5 minutes to reduce the liquid. Remove from heat. Put aside.
4. Use 2 tablespoons of black soy sauce and rub it over the whole duck.
5. Stuff the duck with the prepared stuffing; secure it closed with a bamboo skewer.
6. Add hot water to the roasting pan. Place pan halfway from the bottom of the oven to the rack. Leave it in the heated oven for 45 minutes. Remove from the oven and baste the whole duck with the honey and vinegar mixture.
7. Turn the back side up. Place the duck back in the oven. Reduce the heat to 350 degrees, and bake for 1 hour. Remove from the oven. Baste the whole duck one more time. Turn the duck breast-side up, and bake for 1 more hour. Remove from the oven. Discard the stuffing. Let the duck cool before removing the meat from the bone, and cut it into bite-sized pieces. Garnish with chopped cilantro. Serve with Duck Sauce (page 134) over steamed rice.

Note: Sliced cucumber is also a good companion to this dish.

CHICKEN WITH GINGER (Gai Pahd King)

A suggested dish for my husband whenever he had trouble deciding what to eat. I still remember my mother telling me that ginger is good for my digestion.

4 servings

Ingredients:
½ pound boneless chicken meat, cut into bite-sized pieces
1/3 cup shredded young ginger root
¼ cup shredded prepared wood-ear mushroom
1/3 cup sliced onion
2 green onions, cut into 1½-inch sections
1 teaspoon chopped garlic
½ tablespoon bean sauce
2 tablespoons Emerald Stir-Frying Sauce (page 134)
½ cup chicken broth
¼ teaspoon white ground pepper
2 tablespoons vegetable oil

Method:
1. In a heated cooking pan, add oil, garlic, bean sauce, and ginger root. Stir-fry until the garlic turns light brown.
2. Add chicken. Stir and cook until chicken is almost done.
3. Add onion and wood-ear mushroom. Stir-fry for 1 minute.
4. Add chicken broth, Emerald Stir-Frying Sauce, and white pepper to taste. Stir-fry until it comes to a boil. Cook until the chicken is done.
5. Add green onion. Stir and mix well.
6. Remove from heat. Serve over steamed rice.

Signs

Loving is a sign of security.

Learning is a sign of growth.

Creativity is a sign of intelligence.

Happiness is a sign of satisfaction.

Illness and loss are signs of spiritual need.

Gratitude is a sign of maturity.

Self-discipline is a sign of wisdom.

Giving is a sign of fulfillment.

Compassion is a sign of peace.

Service from the heart is a sign of wholeness.

-Alima Ravadi Quinn

SAUCES

Thai Hot Sauce (Prik Nam Plah)

Peanut Sauce

Emerald Stir-Frying Sauce

Duck Sauce

Emerald House Dressing

Sweet And Sour Sauce

Tamarind Flavored Sauce

THAI HOT SAUCE (Prik Nam Plah)

Thai hot sauce to a Thai, like salt and black pepper to an American. It is very common for a Thai to make a meal out of a bowl of steamed rice, by using this sauce as seasoning.

Ingredients:
1   cup fish sauce
¼   cup fresh hot Thai pepper, chopped
1   tablespoon sugar
¼   cup fresh lime juice

Method:
1. Mix all ingredients.
2. Store in a glass jar for future use. Keep refrigerated. It will last a long time.

PEANUT SAUCE

A favorite comfort dish for Dean, my son-in-law, after he's had a long, hard-working day. All he has to do is just add this sauce to hot steamed rice for a happy meal. This sauce is called for in Chicken Satay (page 55), Bathing Rama (page 81), and Sunshine Rolls (page 65).

Ingredients:
1 can (13.5 oz.) coconut milk
2 tablespoons red curry paste
½ cup sugar (or to taste)
½ cup creamy peanut butter
2 tablespoons tamarind concentrate (now available in Asian markets)
1 teaspoon salt
2 tablespoons vegetable oil
¾ cup water

Method:
1. Heat oil over medium-low heat in a saucepan or wok. Add curry paste and sauté until you can detect the aroma of the curry.
2. Add coconut milk, water, and peanut butter. Mix well. Increase heat to high.
3. Keep stirring until the sauce comes to a boil. Reduce heat to medium-high. Keep stirring until the oil starts to appear on the surface of the sauce. Add sugar, tamarind juice, and salt. Return the mixture to a boil. Keep stirring until the sugar is well-dissolved. Remove from heat. Transfer to a serving bowl.

Note: It is very important to keep stirring the mixture until the sauce is done. Make sure that all ingredients are measured and ready for cooking. The peanut butter can burn fast without stirring, even for a few seconds.

EMERALD STIR-FRYING SAUCE

Recommend you make this sauce at least 2 cups at a time. It is great for marinating and stir-frying in any stir-fried dishes. Oyster by itself is too bland. I always add the Thai seasoning sauce (Thai soy sauce) to add flavor and a little sugar to tone down the salty taste.

Ingredients:
2 cups oyster sauce
2 tablespoons sugar
1 tablespoon Thai soy sauce

Method:
1. Mix all ingredients above. Mix well.
2. Keep sauce mixture in a jar and keep refrigerated for future use.

DUCK SAUCE

Ingredients:
1/3 cup black soy sauce
1 tablespoon Thai soy sauce
1 tablespoon white vinegar
½ tablespoon sugar
1 fresh hot chili pepper, chopped (optional)

Method:
1. Mix all ingredients above.
2. Serve over roast duck.

EMERALD HOUSE DRESSING

Can be used as salad dressing, or as sauce for sunshine rolls.

Ingredients:

1 cup vinegar	1 tablespoon fresh lime juice
1 cup sugar	1 teaspoon salt
1 teaspoon paprika	1 tablespoon fish sauce

Method:
1. In a sauce pan, bring vinegar and sugar to a boil. Stir and mix well.
2. Add salt. Lower heat to low. Simmer until sugar is well-dissolved and it becomes syrup-like. Let cool.
3. Add fish sauce, lime juice, and paprika. Serve over salad, as needed.

SWEET AND SOUR SAUCE

This sauce is served with Emerald Butterflies (page 49) and Thai Spring Rolls (page 43). Some of my customers love this sauce so much they will simply pour it over their entire dinner!

Ingredients:
1 cup sugar
1 cup white vinegar
1 teaspoon salt
1 tablespoon chili sauce

Method:
1. In a small sauce pan, bring vinegar, with sugar, to a boil. Stir and mix well.
2. Add salt. Lower heat and simmer for about 5 minutes, or until the sugar is well-dissolved.
3. Remove from heat. Add chili sauce. Stir and mix well. Cool.
4. Keep in a glass jar for future use.

TAMARIND FLAVORED SAUCE

Can be used for several dishes in Thai cooking. It is used for Pahd Thai (page 77) and Son-In-Law's Eggs (page 111).

Ingredients:
1 cup light brown sugar
1 cup sugar
1 cup white vinegar
1/3 cup tamarind extract (now available in Asian markets)
1½ teaspoon salt

Method:
1. In a saucepan, combine all items. Mix well.
2. Cook over medium-high heat. Bring to a boil.
3. Reduce heat and simmer for 5 minutes or until lightly syrup-like. Stir frequently.
4. Remove from heat. Cool. Transfer the sauce to a glass jar for future use. Keep refrigerated.

DESSERTS AND BEVERAGES

Black Rice Pudding

Fried Banana With Ice Cream

Sticky Rice With Mango

Fruit For Dessert

Thai Iced Tea And Thai Iced Coffee

BLACK RICE PUDDING

The first time for my friend Marilyn O'Brien: this dessert, her description as "a little hug for the soul." It is good for breakfast, too.

8 servings

Ingredients:
½ pound raw black rice
1 can (13.5 oz.) unsweetened coconut milk
2/3 cup + 4 tablespoons sugar
½ teaspoon salt
water for cooking the rice

Method:
1. Wash black rice by rinsing in cold water in a 2-quart saucepan several times until the water is clear. Add water; cover 2 inches above the rice.
2. With high heat, bring the rice to a boil. Stir and cook for 1 minute.
3. Remove from heat. Discard the water. Add the same amount of water to the rice.
4. Bring the rice mixture to a boil again. Stir frequently. Cook until the rice is soft. If the rice is not yet soft and the liquid is getting dry, add more water and cook until the rice has the right consistency.
5. Add 2/3 cup sugar, and bring the mixture to a boil again. Stir and cook for 2 more minutes. Remove from heat.
6. In a small saucepan, heat the coconut milk to a boil. Add 4 tablespoons sugar and ½ teaspoon salt and continue boiling for 1 more minute. Remove from heat. Serve over black rice in individual bowls.

FRIED BANANA WITH ICE CREAM

Very simple to make at home. The contrast of the texture, the crunchy fried banana, wrapped in egg roll wrapper, and the softness of the ice cream, all make it into an exotic dessert.

4 servings

Ingredients:
12 sheets egg roll wrappers
3 medium-sized, firm, ripe bananas
½ cup sugar
2 tablespoons tapioca starch
    vegetable oil for deep frying
    ice cream as needed

Method:
1. Mix the tapioca starch with ½ cup hot water to form a paste to seal the rolls.
2. Cut each banana into halves, and then quarters. Discard the peels.
3. Put the sugar on a plate, spread out evenly.
4. Coat each piece of banana with sugar, 1 piece at a time, and wrap each piece in an egg roll wrapper, the same way as wrapping Thai Spring Rolls *(see illustrations on pages 44 and 45)*. Seal with tapioca paste.
5. Deep-fry in hot oil 350-375 degrees until golden brown.
6. Remove from oil. Place the fried banana on a paper towel on a serving platter. Serve with ice cream.

STICKY RICE WITH MANGO

Asked my daughter Suzanne what her comfort food was at the Emerald. Sticky Rice with Mango was her answer. This is a seasonal dessert for Thai restaurants in the USA, but a year-round popular dessert in Thailand. It is not a home-made dessert in Thailand, as it is available all the time from food vendors and is also inexpensive.

4 servings

Ingredients:
1 cup long grain sweet rice
2 ripe mangoes (They must be in season - out of season's no good!)
1 can (13.5 oz.) coconut milk
¼ cup sugar
1 teaspoon salt

Method:
1. Soak rice in warm water for 3-5 hours.
2. Wash well and drain.
3. Wrap the rice in clean cheesecloth, and steam in a steamer. With boiling water in the bottom of the steamer, steam for 20 minutes or until the rice is cooked. (The rice should look clear.)
4. A few minutes before the rice is done, heat the coconut milk, sugar, and salt together in a small saucepan. Boil for 1 minute. Remove from heat.
5. Mix the coconut milk with rice in a large mixing bowl. Cover for 20 minutes. Stir with a spoon and compact it before dishing it out for individual servings.
6. Serve with slices of ripe mango.

Note: If you enjoy sticky rice, you may want to own a sticky rice steamer, imported from Thailand. Now it is available in most Asian markets. Instead of cheesecloth, you can put the rice directly into the bamboo basket. Dip the basket in cold water before use.

FRUIT FOR DESSERT

Aaaah, fruit for dessert. Friends have recommended to me to talk about the science of nutrition and the body, or perhaps to refer directly in my book to Buddha's teachings. But there are hundreds of books available on scientific nutrition, Buddha's philosophy, the Ayurveda, eating right for your blood type, etc. To me, the circle of life is very important when feeding the soul.

Fruit is a natural dessert, provided by Mother Earth and the hard-working orchard keepers. When I have the opportunity, in the summer, I always enjoy going to a big, nearby orchards and picking my own fruit, when thay are in season. These include my favorites: Rainier cherries in mid-June, Donut peaches in mid-July, and Fuji apples in October. I also enjoy the grapefruit from Texas, when it is in peak season, as well as Satsuma oranges from California between Thanksgiving and Christmas.

As well, I enjoy my favorite blueberries during peak season from the farmers' market near where I live. With all the fresh fruit I consume during peak season, my body never asks for processed fruit juice, avoiding all that excess sugar in my body. I believe that our bodies get the most nutrients from different kinds of fruit during their peak seasons. It is also less expensive to buy from the farmers' market, or from the U-Pick orchards. Fresh fruit has a pretty long life in the refrigerator.

I still remember when I took Dara and Billy to visit my mother in Thailand. Dara was 5, and Billy was only 18 months. It was during the peak mango season. My mother took her time peeling a ripe mango to feed both of them. I could tell how happy her grandchildren were. I have started doing the same thing with my grandchildren, too. We go to the orchard together every summer for seasonal fruits.

Thai fruit is bountiful and fresh all year round. I missed Thai fruit more than anything else when I first came to the USA in 1972. Then I was introduced to U-Pick apple orchards and different U-Pick berry orchards when we lived in Washington D.C., and later on in Kent, Washington. In this book, I am very happy to show you pictures of some exotic Thai fruit from Thailand, to remind you that you need fresh fruit in your diet.

THAI ICED TEA AND THAI ICED COFFEE

Ingredients:
1/3 cup Thai tea leaves or Thai ground coffee beans (can be purchased at Asian market)
10 cups water
½-1 cup sugar to taste
half-and-half cream, as needed
ice cubes, as needed

Method:
1. In a large saucepan, bring water to a boil.
2. Stir in Thai tea leaves or Thai coffee beans (already ground). Boil the mixture for 5 minutes, stirring occasionally.
3. Remove from heat. Strain liquid with cheesecloth (can be purchased at Asian market). Heat the liquid to a boil again. Add sugar, stirring until dissolved. Serve hot, or cold over ice, with half-and-half cream. Keep refrigerated.

Note: If you cannot find the cheesecloth, use a coffee filter instead. It may take a little longer to process.

Full Cycle

I didn't know I was in this world
Until I realized I had a body.
All I knew was, I had a heart to love.

I didn't know I had a mind
Until I got caught doing something not quite right.
All I knew was, I had a heart to love.

I didn't know life would be so strange and difficult
Until I left the bosom of my family.
All I knew was, I had a heart to love.

I didn't know there were so many religions
Until some of them claimed me.
All I knew was, I had a heart to love.

I didn't know I had so much to sacrifice
Until I had a family of my own.
All I knew was, I had a heart to love.

I didn't know there were so many challenges
Until I followed my duties to their ends.
All I knew was, I had a heart to love.

I didn't know there were such things as joy and peace
Until I held my newborn grand-daughter in my arms.
All I knew was, love had embraced my heart.

-Alima Ravadi Quinn

REFLECTION ON THAI FOOD AND SUFISM

Thai food is like a bowl of beautiful elements, which are used by different cultures in different forms of cooking, and from which the Thai people borrow, integrating them with an open heart.

Sufism is like a bowl of wisdom which the Sufis have borrowed from different religions in the world and put into practice in their daily lives with an open heart.

I'd like to start by telling you my own personal experience with different religions before I knew that I was a Sufi.

I was raised with Taoist principles by my Chinese parents. They taught me by their natural way of living as responsible, kind, and loving human beings with their family, friends, and neighbors.

For my education, however, they sent me to Catholic schools. The last four and a half years were in Australia, where I became certified as an elementary school teacher. When I returned to Thailand, I continued as a parochial school teacher. I also joined the Catholic Church when I was twenty-five. I experienced God's love and His presence for the first time when I was baptized.

Four years later I fell in love and agreed to marry an American civil servant/diplomat, for whose children I had been serving as governess. He was a Unitarian Universalist. The Divine gift of love has enabled me to raise his children to adulthood, along with our two children, with whom love has blessed us.

Later, at age 45, I was inspired to join the "UU" church myself. It was at this church that I learned about Sufism from a speaker who gave a Sunday service in 1995. She turned out to be a Sufi teacher herself. As I worked with her, I found that I myself was a Sufi and felt very much at home.

I have learned that Sufism is a way of living which is activated by God's love. Sufism has enabled me to capture the wisdom from different religions with an open mind and open heart. It is just like having a delicious meal to satisfy my being which brings joy and happiness to myself and others around me.

ABOUT THE AUTHOR

I remember an assignment, in grade school, in which you were supposed to describe someone that you admired: your idol. Mother Theresa, the President, and any member of Duran Duran were among the persona represented by my classmates. I, however, chose a diamond, as yet, undiscovered by the rest of the world, my mother Ravadi.

She has been my idol ever since I could comprehend the term (minus, of course, some brief moments in my teenage years). Now, Alima Ravadi Lekprichakul Quinn is still the most inspiring, loving, energetic, positive person whom I have ever met.

I feel blessed that I am the offspring of this wonderful lady. The publication of this book continues to inspire me as did her work on her first cookbook -- "Joy of Thai Cooking" -- and her mystical book of poems entitled "The Wings of My Soul." (You should read it!)

What to tell of Ravadi? Where she comes from does not matter (so I've learned), as much as who she is. She was born to Chinese/Thai immigrant parents, near Bangkok, Thailand. Her father was a heck of a business man, going from millionaire to bankruptcy more than once. Ravadi attended school at a convent in Melbourne, Australia. She protected her sisters from the wrath of the less lovable nuns and became very close to Mother Marie Therese, who had quite an influence on her life.

Later, with her teacher's certificate, Ravadi became a school teacher in Thailand. Then, she was hired as a governess for a divorced American man working for the U.S. Department of Defense. The children fell in love with Miss Ravadi ("The Sound of Music," anyone?). The rest is history. Garry Quinn brought his new wife and family (the children, Amy, Suzy, and Jim) back to the States, where he worked with the Government and with Boeing on both coasts. It was in the States that Billy and Dolly were born.

While living in Western Washington, Ravadi helped with the inception of one of the Northwest's very first Thai restaurants, in the late 70s. Later, after the family relocated to Richland, Washington, sister Sunanta and Ravadi opened the Emerald of Siam Thai Restaurant, which has thrived for the past 25 years.

Mom's (Ravadi's) passion for providing a family-like atmosphere, and food prepared with love, and the traditional spices of exotic Thai cuisine, created a menu "to die for." With over 60 items to choose from, I have never tired of eating there-- and I've been eating at the Emerald for over 25 years. The food is healthy, tastes great, and looks beautiful. There is nothing else one could ask for. When you put together Mom's conceptions of love, mind, body, and food, it's no wonder that her restaurant has become a place of nourishment and therapy for many.

Please enjoy Mom's book. Her inspiration has warmed many hearts and palates, and hopefully yours.

Dara (Dolly) Mae Therese Quinn

We Share

(A Reflection On Diversity)

You and I walk different paths
 But we share the same destination.

You and I live in different forms
 But we share the same elements.

You and I have different wills
 But we share the same bliss of God.

You and I have different desires
 But we share the same need for compassion.

You and I experience different fears and pains
 But we share the same roots of healing.

You and I have different gifts of intelligence
 But we share the same privilege of being human.

You and I have different mothers
 But we share the same abundance of Mother Earth.

You and I have different faiths and traditions
 But we share the same Spirit of Love and Guidance.

You and I create different illusions to make sense out of our lives
 But we share the same Truth that brings Joy and Peace.

-Alima Ravadi Quinn